11 Things to Celebrate Before Breakfast

Ruth Broyde Sharone   **Leah Broyde Abrahams**

©2025 Ruth Broyde Sharone and Leah Broyde Abrahams
Title: 11 Things to Celebrate Before Breakfast

All rights reserved. No part of this publication may be reproduced or transmitted in a form or by any means, electronic or mechanical, including photocopy, recording, or information storage and retrieval system now known or to be invented, without permission in writing from the publisher, except by a reviewer who wishes to quote brief passages in connection with a print, online, or broadcast review.

Published by: Global Peace Publications
www.LeahAbrahamsPhotography.com

Author: Ruth Broyde Sharone
Photographer: Cover and internal photographs by Leah Broyde Abrahams
Cover design and book design by Jason Davis
Manufactured in the United States of America.

First Edition

10 9 8 7 6 5 4 3 2 1

Paperback ISBN: 978-0-9992563-1-2

*To our parents, Raya and Samuel Broyde,
who taught us to live life with passion.*

1

I am alive.

It's a new day.

I am not alone.

The world was made for me–and all living things.

I was made from stardust and will return to stardust.

I am an original.

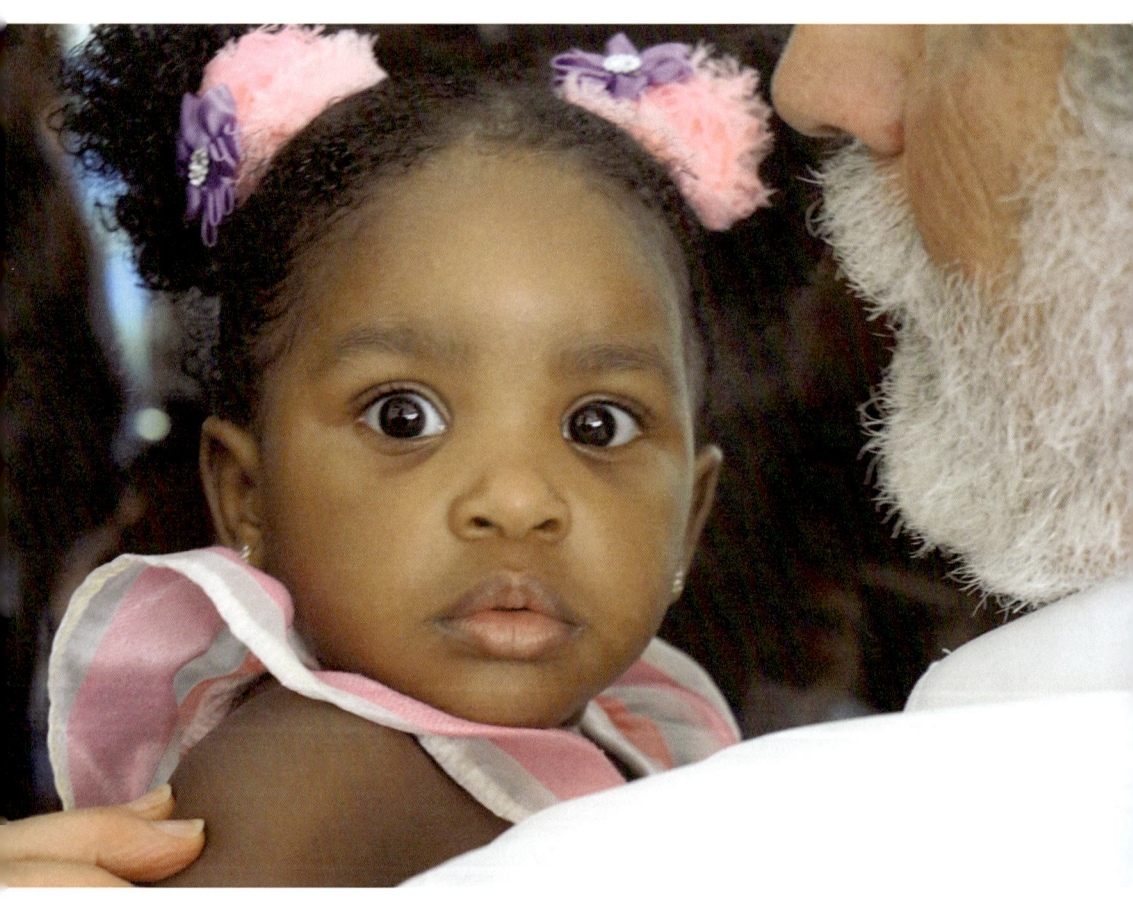

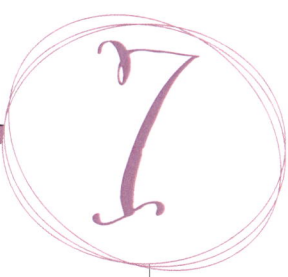

I can choose
my destiny.

I am my brother's and sister's keeper.

Life is an invitation.

Whatever the question,
the answer is love.

This one is left blank for you to fill in.

The number **11** has been interpreted for many centuries as a portal to divine intuition, knowledge, and higher consciousness, a belief held by the Mayans and by other ancient cultures as well.

Some people believe the number **11** is obvious in the ancient visual depiction of Thoth, the Egyptian god of writing, intellectual pursuits, and magical knowledge. Often Thoth is depicted as a man with the head of an ibis bird and he wears a headdress that forms the number **11** on his chest.

In China, **11** represents balance and reflects the Yin-Yang aspect of the universe. In the deck of Tarot cards, **11** represents justice and truth.

According to numerologists – who believe numbers and letters hold energy that influences our life and destiny– the number **11** is highly significant, and is considered a "Master Number," along with 22 and

33, capable of initiating big changes in our life. Master numbers are also thought of as master teachers, to wake us up to what is possible when we can't see it on our own.

In modern times, many people around the world have come to attribute special spiritual significance to the exact time **11:11**, especially when it appears on a digital clock. They may refer to it as the "Angel number." It's God's way of saying "Hello," believers say, to give us encouragement, and to remind us of our divine connection. It has also been described as a symbolic union of time and space, where the real and the surreal intersect.

We decided to promote **11** ideas in our book because we are hoping that once you read the first 10 things we have chosen to celebrate before breakfast, you will come up with your own unique **11**th celebration—one that leads you to greater awareness and a deeper appreciation for the gift of life.

About The Author

Ruth Broyde Sharone is a veteran filmmaker/journalist/author and the creator of MEET ME THERE, the Interfaith Musical, an exuberant celebration of our cultural and religious diversity (www.interfaiththemusical.com). Ruth wrote, produced, and directed the prize-winning documentary "God and Allah Need to Talk," which has been screened on college campuses across the U.S. and around the world. Her interfaith memoir, *Minefields & Miracles*, received multiple literary awards and more than 30 testimonials from religious leaders including H.H. the Dalai Lama. She also contributed more than 50 articles to *The Interfaith Observer*. Ruth now lives in Los Angeles.

About The Photographer

Leah Broyde Abrahams is a passionate photographer whose work has been juried into many exhibitions and who has had several one-woman shows. After a career in program evaluation and research, while contributing as a leader in volunteerism in Green Bay, Wi, she created Mixed Media Memoirs, a publishing company. She has produced a number of videos and more than 35 books. Her editing and ghostwriting brought her great satisfaction and today her primary focus is photography. Her photobook *Do You See What I See?* was selected into the National Photobook Exhibition of 2023. Leah now lives in Boston. (www.LeahAbrahamsPhotography.com)